BREATHING IN THE DARK

Borderland

There is a mystic borderland
That lies just past the limits of our
    work-a-day world,
And it is peopled with the friends
    we met and loved
A year, a month, a week ago, and parted
    from with aching hearts —
Yet knew that we must lose the touch
    of hand on hand
And only clasp the thread of memory.
But so near do we feel this land,
So sure are we that those same hearts
    are true,
That when in waking dreams there comes
    a call
That sets the thread of memory aglow —
We know that just by stretching out our
    hand
In written word of love, or book, or
    flower —
The waiting hand will clasp our own
    once more
Across the silence in the same old way.

— Clementine Newman

Breathing in the Dark

◖◗

poems

to Bruce,
cousin & fellow the word
practitioner of mention a
(not to mention a
great chef!)
Cheers,
Susan
Luther Reunion
Oct. 2006

Susan Luther

◖ *banyon swamp creek press*

Banyon Swamp Creek Press is an imprint of Centurion Publishers,
P. O. Box 248, Hazel Green, Alabama 35750.

Publisher's Cataloging-in-Publication Data

Luther, Susan Militzer.
Breathing in the Dark : poems / Susan Luther.

p. cm.
ISBN 0-9673919-1-1 (alk. paper)
1. American Poetry.   2. Southern States—Poetry.
I. Title.
PS3562.U875B74 2000   811'.54—DC21   00-190696

Typeface: Comic Sans MS, Footlight MT Light

Printed and bound in the United States of America
by Thomson-Shore, Inc.

First printing

The paper in this book meets the guidelines for permanence and
durability of the Committee on Production Guidelines for Book
Longevity of the Council on Library Resources. ∞

acknowledgements

I am grateful to Patricia Carrigan for allowing her art *(Things That Stay)* to appear on the jacket cover of this book, and to the Vermont Studio Center for the fellowship that acquainted us with each other.

I also thank the editors who chose these poems for publication in the following journals: *Birmingham Poetry Review*, "Red Plaid, Black Coffee & a No. 3," "Silver Streak"; *Bloodroot*, "Afterlife," "After Sylvia"; *California Quarterly*, "Table Talk with Spaghetti"; *Concerning Poetry*, "The Guests"; *Cumberland Poetry Review*, "After Many Disappointments: Many Deaths" (as "Seventeen Months After One Death and Seven Months After Another"), "Small Lyric *als Abschied*"; *draconian measures*, "The FDA Report on Cellulite," "Legacy," *"pour la fille au cheveux de lin"*; *Elk River Review*, "Cure," "Nuya Saligugi"; *Green River Review*, "Suicides"; *Half Tones to Jubilee*, "Reading, for Distraction" (as "Reading the Text"); *Kalliope*, "Poesia" (as "Invoking the Muse"), "Revocation," "Valedictory" (as "To a Young Friend"); *Kansas Quarterly*, "Rain: Too Much to Say"; *The MacGuffin*, "Delectation"; *The Malahat Review*, "Revolution: Flashback"; *Noccalula*, "Anything worth doing is worth doing badly, " "Engagement," "Ugly"; *Number One*, "Amanuensis," "Mutability," "Snake Handlers," "Vista" (as "Finding a Vista Within"), "The world is a dangerous neighborhood"; *Piedmont Literary Review*, "Skeletons; Closets"; POEM, "Doll Museum," "Two Views of Howard's Chapel"; *St. Andrews Review*, "Hiatus," "The Marriage"; *The Scribbler*, "Requiem (Remembering Vardamon)"; *Slant*, "After Her Father's Death," "Nightrider"; *Small Pond*, "Traveling (via?) Iceland"; *Sonoma Mandala*, "Alice in Gray" (as "Alice, Aging"); *Waterways*, "Nailed in the Bush"; *Yellow Silk*, "Sheaves." "Of Another Stripe" appears in SKUNK (Jumping Cholla Press); "Two Views of Howard's Chapel" was reprinted in *Alabama Poets: A Contemporary Anthology* (Livingston University Press). "Afterlife" was reprinted in *Gold Dust.* "Ugly" was reprinted in *Alabama Horizons* (Mulberry River Press) and in the National Association for Poetry Therapy's original poem chapbook.

Most of my mother's poems quoted here were published in 1930-31 issues of *The Distaff*: *Spinner of Yarns*, the literary journal of Florida State College for Women ("Return," "Cinquain," "Query," and, from the sequence "Camp Flastacowo": "The Bathers," "The Arrival," "On the Road," "Around the Fire" and "Lights Out"). Typed copies of "Borderland" (unsigned) and "November Enchantment" (signed) were inserted in her composition book; I do not know whether they were published.

◑

As Dr. Johnson wrote, "I have protracted my work, till most [at least, far too many] of those whom I wished to please have sunk into the grave." I thank them in spirit, and you, who remain, in these words. I hope you will find them a small return on all you have given me. Especially I thank Robert Luther, for believing in the work, for believing (and repeating when I need to hear it) that "poets are the keepers of the language."

to the memory of Clementine Newman Militzer (1911-1976)
who moved from liveoak sand to prairie dirt
and gave me words

◀ ◀

▶ ▶
and to the memory of Walter Ernest Militzer (1906-1984)
who left to me his love of science, art, critters
and punny jokes

Root and Branch

Too late, to identify the tree I took for granted
summers by the creek; or home, on morning walks
(for who's to say if the two in ignorance I thought alike
were in fact the same?)

The tree at home stood behind a house on my daily route
before pines I hadn't noticed; each season I looked
up, its — catkins? and true green overflew them on the wind.

Were its leaves simple or pinnate? Smooth or toothed?
No photograph, no shard of bark, rewards inattention.
And the *Field Guide's* too imprecise for novice work,
absent the specimen. Pinckneya? Hornbeam? Pignut hickory?

A stranger told me; I didn't write it down.
Receive, page, instead the names of its late-revealed relation,
pine, and those a stone's throw from the picnic table,
gazebo, the front porch: *cypress, redbud, hackberry,*
dogwood, scarlet maple, cherry laurel, pin oak,
willow oak, sweetgum, black cherry, sycamore.

As for you — add to their honor roll *ghost*
lost when I heard the oh-familiar *drummer down* tree-cutting
down.

Now in spring no more will I read
your weft of bloom, weaving in
the breeze; nor scent the path of brief-born
mysteries — but I will
remember you; I'll remember you. ◖▶

To the Reader

Your poem must *eternal* be,
    Dear sir!—it cannot fail—
For 'tis incomprehensible,
    And wants both *head* and *tail*.
                    — S. T. COLERIDGE

"The wish to survive, / . . . is, I believe, the deepest human wish," writes Louise Glück (in "Lute Song," from *Vita Nova*). If so, and I too believe it is so, how impossible to contemplate the volumes on volumes of dead letters without falling into a kind of crumbling, leather-bound despair. (Not to mention that, even in the best of worlds, even if we humans do not war or pollute ourselves off this blue planet, "forever" will or may last only until the explosion of our star.)

Nevertheless, there may be more than wisdom in leaving no earthly trace. Humans change as the view from my back window changes, presenting one moment a cottontail nibbling the unmown grass or a Carolina wren dirt-bathing in a flower pot; the next, a neighbor's cat. But verse (for instance) preserves all our moral and aesthetic embarrassments, so long as there's ink to the page — and even one reader willing to make sense of it.

Which is partly why it's so difficult to tell the truth. However, although I am now years removed from the woman who composed most of them and the personae who speak them, the verses here tried to do that, tried to voice something of her, their (and necessarily my own, and, one hopes, beyond my own) mind and heart. Because of this, because they represent certain truths or movements carried forward from the past, I have altered some of them from their earlier, published versions for the sake of readability, but only insofar as seemed compatible with their original terms. I have not altered their perspectives nor their modes, which range from high to low.

No one can know how another will respond to her work. But whoever you are, however this book came into your hand, I hope you will find something here of kinship, even joy. Who else have I written it for but you?

◖◗ *Huntsville, Alabama*

ix

Contents

◀▶ *Coyote, I call you*

cure
◀◀◀◀◀◀

night song
◀◀◀◀◀◀◀◀◀◀◀

◀ ● ▶ So much of you survives

a marriage
◀◀◀◀◀◀◀◀◀

husband death
▶▶▶▶▶▶▶▶▶▶▶

Return

◖◗

You have come back.
How and why it is I do not know
Yet the sound of your voice,
Eager as a bird's song at dawn,
Has struck an answering note
On the string I thought broken
Long ago.
I shall keep my wonder-filled heart close hid
Lest the harsh rasp
Of my questioning
Drown the whisper of your return.

—CLEMENTINE NEWMAN

◖ Amanuensis

◖◖◖◖◖◖◖◖◖◖◖◖◖

▶▶▶▶▶▶▶▶▶▶▶

somebody's vacant dreamhouse
◀◀◀◀◀◀◀◀◀◀◀◀◀◀◀◀◀◀◀◀◀◀◀

The Bathers

Sun rays slant
On glistening bodies
Poised
Tip-toe
On the edge
Of a wooden plank.
　　　　　—Clementine Newman

Legacy

In a blue dress V'd
   to the cleft
for an Occasion

I once announced to a scholarly
honoree: "I think I'll write a paper
on the Fatal Woman." "Oh?" — a sniff —

"You fancy yourself
as Sexton, La Belle Dame
sans Merci?"

I was miffed, then later
conceded . . . *too*

true: all those dance cards
(Anne) from high school, filled
with names — ribbons, roses —
love letters and broken hearts

in spite of the father who said
acne literally made him
      sick. Then
babies, husbands, lovers — and
breakdowns — but why trouble
you with details, news of fugues?

Read the poems I write, I write,
I write, and all

for you . . . For the hoodwinked bird
   that covets our entrails, for the
   freedom of being no god

(At the beach last summer
my husband and I fed crows
on the balcony, one so glossy
its feathers looked dewed: but its feet
   involved in fisherman's twine
pecked into desperate knots. At first
the others wouldn't let it eat; but it
persisted at odd hours, finding crumbs.
Finally we almost got close enough to scissor
the filaments, put bread in its beak.

Years later, I still wonder whether or how
long the bird lived, ask myself

the same unyielding questions
about love; survival

and can still find
only these redeeming

images:
                    The balcony. The blessed wafer. Blue
                    dresses. Names, memories. Wings.

                    The fingers. *The line.*)

Revocation

Art is History's nostalgia.
— Derek Walcott

Come Kalliope, come Mnemosyne,
Erato, Polyhymnia, you of the golden brow
and lyre, Euterpe, Thalia, Terpsichore,
Urania, breathe with me now; Klio,
Melpomene, come. Disturb my prime
as Poesy persecuted Keats:

as you woke Hesiod on the hill,
as your will dictated Homer,
as the Daughters of Beulah in-
nerved Blake. What matter
if you are shadows, bones
leached dry by the bliss of time? What matter

if this — rhyme, even verse itself — is nothing
but some *shibboleth* of terms past?
Your hereafter still teases
out words, paint, and stone:
Dr. Jung could not ignore you;
Akhmatova — and I — implore you.
Coleridge importuned you by name,
Deagon shames you into lightning —
for your sake, history itself grows
wistful. *"Their music, which once was
the harmony of the spheres, has ceased
to sound"* — Muses! —

Who dare prose that you are dead?

Present your lovely heads anent the sliding glass door
that leads to the patio, star sisters, appear
in the microwave, walk through the wall.
Klio, Thalia: I call you
to answer — what human

invented you? Come, bring us
your laurels and lutes, fair illusion,
mint from the garden, whatever

trifle will do. Sly device, nine-
        lived metaphor:

whatever you hunger
for. *Come.*

Revolution: Flashback

Extremists can be artistic, according to Bo Gritz, sometime presidential candidate, who expressed sympathy for the Oklahoma City victims and then called the bombing "a masterpiece of science and art — a Rembrandt."
— Pat Truly, "Responsibility of free speech," *N.Y. Times News Service* (1995)

Sept. 11, 1976 —

A plane is hijacked
by 'liberators' pleading freedom
who have placed a bomb in New York City,
who demand publication of their demands
in four major newspapers.

The New York City Police, meanwhile,
defuse the bomb (except for one
who got too close
when the bomb went off, spilling
its slag odor as energy, a force
blank and colorless,
impacted the man) —

No grand explosion of semen here
(the professor expands).

No young man's instrument seeking the queen,
no old man usurped by the authoritarian
blaze of youth: no Marie Antoinette raped. This
is no organic thing breeding coup in the universe
of Fogeys. It is a Mechanism.
Here there is no Satan.
There is no Orc.

There is merely a black box
designed by colorless young men their captives call
"Civilized, gracious of manner." There is no
blood; no fire;

but the casualties *are* few. The four papers
dutifully report; the demands are met; and,
on the whole, there are only these

dead: one policeman,
the fire of Orc,
Marie Antoinette,
too many children
and one well-oiled bomb.

pour la fille au cheveux de lin

i

Knock-kneed before a lecture
I'd been disgusted for months
    I'd agreed to give

I answered your mother's "Are you
    scared?" with

'You bet I am — I'm
terrified!' "Don't feel

alone" — she told me — then disclosed that
you, the studious one, have decided
to enter a beauty contest but now
have more than minimal doubts.
So now, having parsed the topic
without losing the page, or my voice —

ii

What can I say to cheer you,
you whom I can only describe
by referring the observer to a melody
by Debussy, knowing even that's
just an easy allusion at odds

with your elusiveness, the surprise
I always feel when I find out something
astonishing about you, such as this?

13

iii

You *are* beautiful. You are Yourself.

Standing tall, stepping light
    as a fawn, pale
hair drawn back and up —

if those judges have even half taste,
    cher fille,
    you'll win hands

iv

down, and in contests more demanding
        of your grace.

(Nobody believes me, either, when I complain
I feel gelatinous. They laugh
in my face when I say I need
good luck. You, however, like
your mother, have always understood

why I still get stage fright
every time I have to perform,
could hardly croak the solos chosen
for two sisters' weddings, don't quite know

how I managed the aisle and steps up
at another ceremony without going down
or over in my heels, have no idea how I stayed on my feet
the however-long time my lecture lasted,

am amazed sometimes to be in this world at all, even,
when I really think about it, but can concede that
Something thus far has propelled and propped me
whenever I asked it to, even those times when, dizzy
with grief or fright, ludicrously ready to faint,
I've been primed with excuses such as
'I've only recently gotten over the flu' or
It must be something I ate.

The show *has* gone on. Which it would do
and will do, eventually, without me. For now,
though, I'm just glad to know I'm not alone,

glad that something has kept me
going, whatever we call it:

Confidence, maybe, if we think of it
as a *con;* or love. Cantankerousness.)

Good Luck.

for Katherine

Doll Museum
(Jekyll Island)

Pretending to be children
or at least impersonating parents
of children left with aunts
in such cities as Mobile

we step into a postcard cottage large enough
(it seems) to house the miniaturized population of
London: buying admission from the lady at the desk

whose blue hairdo nods:

she has seen us before
— may be one of us herself,
crooning to her darlings in the secret
bloom of night, smoothing Betty's hair,
straightening a bisque head's dress.

Glass cases display more dolls than you would think
            to count: too busy saluting
Poor Pitiful Pearl, Madame Alexanders,
Barbie's precocious bodice and hobbly heels —
Shirley Temple and the Dionne quints *(We could get*
        a mint for them now, someone whispers, *if Mom*
            hadn't given your old set, remember? to the poor kids
                    at the orphanage)

— all sizes, nations, costumes, ages,
from last year's craze to saint sirens
whose cotton bodies decay beneath
china faces, scarlet lips
parted as if to kiss or speak
over pearly, everlasting teeth.

Even the fairytale dollhouse is a little girl's marvel —
every detail perfect, right down to the w. c.

Later, we walk the village outside
where storybook millionaires
once arranged their furniture

        — lifesized
but empty, as though carpenters or elves
had sweltered at their labors for months,
but all the Jennies and Sallies formerly
breathless for Christmas grew up

in a single fortnight, all at once
too knowing to confess so outré a preference
as dolls — so that now the houses must be

restored. One, your favorite,
      stands untenanted

but with a fresh coat of paint
on the door, as if the toymaker
had only just left for tea.

A plastic envelope in an album
keeps the picture you took of me

           there, on the doubled staircase
           of somebody's vacant dreamhouse

hair, eyelashes, breasts
      just so.

The Guests

*. . . drawn
to law as to starlight
late guests sift voices
from the cricket-haunted night.*
　　　　—*Jane Marston ("Open House")*

I wear décolleté brown silk,
conscious of being over thirty,
faintly desperate to show off
while I may, before the flesh I'm made of shrinks
　　　　and strings.

The fringes of grandmother's silk shawl spill
　　　　across my shoulders
to the floor;

through the open door shimmer laughter and lights.

We enter the festal chamber.

Presently a shining woman, dressed entirely
in satin green, healthy, emerald, radiant,
greets me; her naturally crimson cheeks
　　　　belie the hungering disease
discovered months before
that feeds on her bright bosom.
We speak of music, decorations.

And we drift to the table, richly laden;
my husband eats, approves, expands,
genial in talk (and forgets, just days ago
he shouted out in nightmare; forgets
　　　　the nameless horrors
of his dream-stunned sleep) — leans

18

to catch a syllable,
touches a hand, warms
as he holds fast the hand
of the celebrated guest

whose charm inspires this amorous occasion,
who is most beloved among the revelers,
who seems so young yet

(though I have seen,
     when he has bent
to kiss a child's offered forehead,
the tender scalp encroaching pinkly).

One black-clad apparition drinks alone
in a corner, stale as death. Oblivious,
     the men and women crowd
     about the viands on the table,
touch, smile, savor, touch; as from the threshold
of my gaze approaches — vaguely stumbling —

one who, painfully innocent, aches
to feast upon some miracle of silk
and cleavage, to pluck a leaf
          of Angel crust
     from my unbound hair.

the muse who disappeared
◖◖◖◖◖◖◖◖◖◖◖◖◖◖◖◖◖

The Arrival
◖◗
One last curve,
An open gate,
And the lake—burnished bronze shot with gold—
Glitters before us.
                    —*Clementine Newman*

Valedictory
for Sibyl

You wear white lace,
a graduation dress cut
to a pattern I found

in a magazine, thinking it
          looked like you,
and your naturally-pale blonde hair

(unlike my own, which, at your age,
I peroxided whiter) sheens
the pearl complexion which,
at your age, I also yearned for.

And I have made other mistakes
as well, not only wanted to be
what I never was, but tried not to be

what I must. Impossible, thus, not to see
likenesses, not to seek resemblances;
like any wayward parent, not to read

myself not only in the taste for sentiment
and lace I know we share, or love

of your mother, your sister
and your father. All this

and greater age
make me consider it my right
to tell you now

how beautiful you are,
how like and unlike them,
how like and unlike myself,

how precious, how apparently fragile
in your bright eagerness, yet how capable
of making exactly your own fortune
and your own mistakes.

Dowry

(Camagüey, 1905)

I begin to feel that I want to know that the center of the earth is burning — melting hot. —Georgia O'Keeffe

●

It is not the way
they told it, corazón —

no, the day I died

the sky rang clear
as a bell of thunder:

nothing written on the morning

but the mountains scribed
across the valley, a pencil
of fog dividing the palms . . . no gift

of price but dawn, ablaze
as with the fire of all the saints.

Four years — What was I to do?

I left the niños — your uncles — with Madre Inez
and I went to him, alone on the campaña.

Before we knew our names again

      the sun rose high
and it was time
      to ride the long way home

through the swaying fields, through the field

of old Don Fulgencio, our neighbor then,
plowing the rocky ground his father left him
with the single ox and stake he always drove.
Andrés had told me: after comida, he and Felipe
would break ground beside our house

with the new blades just come by ship
from Louisiana, each taking
four yoke to draw. When the hour came

I took my needle to the window
    where I could watch them
but something happened — perhaps I did
die — perhaps I only dreamed —

        I did not see Felipe fall
        nor Andrés try to pull the team back

but dreamed I was flying
up the Maestra

and down, down the mountain

                • •

        into the sea . . .

        where coral beds
        red as carnelian

        swam with fish
        of bright citrine

enameled with
obsidian drops,
      floating

   into the shadow

of the montaña . . . *Mi Maria!*

      — I would have
cried, but I could not
      cry out —

     ● ● ●

and then — a narrow
passageway . . . I ran

between steep rocks
whose broad thumbs

caught my mantón
on their rough wet skin,

unwinding distances
     below
  until an eye of

fire

unbowed
the darkness:

into
arcs untold

of flame, blue
spires, rivers

a lake a cave
the burning

lava
of a song: *blessed*

> *Art thou*
> *among*

women . . . on the other side
of dusk

a fountain of marble
snow
the streaming

cloak of the Virgin . . .

(— *tonta, despierta!* —)

Then someone
was pulling at

these pearls

・・・・

in my ear:
   Ai! José! José,
   Is that you?

— But the crazy thief jumped

out the open window and ran
away — and I woke up

 in a coffin
in my wedding dress

 into a life
I didn't know I'd left

that so soon became
your mother's life,

your other uncles' lives, our lives
together — and this new life you go to

corazón, though we may never see you
again

so far away: for the sake of our love,
you must take these pearl-and-diamond drops
  Felipe had given us

when he came home to the farm
and I met Papa's beautiful brother

half a decade after the war — sign of the *abuela*
whose words you must give to your own daughter

> *flaming   as the breath   of sunshine*
> *changing   as the night   of Bellamar*

and granddaughter, mi querida:
even as you must tell them how
        the sun of Maestra

calls, the stars'
fingers beckon
and Venus casts
her blue shadow,
night bursts
into silver flame

or sunsets weave
cloth-of-gold
upon the loom
of clouds, sunrise
curves the whole sky
into a crimson jewel,
summer rains rush down
to wash and hide the fields
of cane — and you must tell them
        I did not know how I could live without him

you remember me.

Amanuensis
for S.C.N.

I wasn't satisfied with the outcome
of your life — not satisfied with safe passage
(which, I now believe, you too may not have had).

Now I read your youthful journal
and think "I could have written this":
thought the same thoughts,

perhaps used the same words.
Do we never belong to ourselves,
we daughters? For your aims therein

were always mine and are mine still,
the demand "My formless poems
need a pattern," that singing tinnitus

that is never still — yet when you married
you never wrote again, simply
let a little girl read your early poems,

wrote down her first verse
when she wasn't old enough to write,
somehow bequeathed her the muse

who disappeared beneath the magnolias,
the marble, the must, the moss
fallen from trees inside Oak Ridge's iron

gates, falling
on grandmother's front lawn.

Pearls

for M.J.V.

Margaret speaks skillet, the dialect
of wildflowers & birds. How to strain
yogurt to make nonfat yogurt "cheese,"
a way to make whipped topping
out of nonfat dry milk,
how much cholesterol in salmon,
a recipe for sugarless apple cake.

We've been friends for years
but rarely mention bugbears
such as diabetes, the walking
breakdown that knocked me off
my feet almost but didn't, how badly
Dad's death scared her. We know what falls
to the knife, alright, but when you've pared
as much as we have, the cookbook means

more than *sauté, chop, dice, mince*
or *fold in the eggwhites.* So today,
taking our tea outside, we talk
menus, the meal Margaret's fixing
Thursday for 4 generations, her
weekly family night. We listen

to the road noise on Governor's,
watch chickadees bussing chicks
in the birdhouse. A chipmunk
spooks 2 mourning doves. As wrens
drop in & out of the red ceramic bottle
too high for the cats to jump at,
furnished with branch they've used
2 years now, mooring, instead
of *love* we speak of "wild" things,
the walk we just took in the woods,
Indian pink, the Carolinas she's lured
back nesting one more spring beside
us on Margaret's upstairs porch.

The FDA Report on Cellulite

Fat is an expression of personal power.
— Meadow & Weiss

comes in the mail today.
I read it avidly
for justification, find

"Where there is no obesity
there is no so-called cellulite."
(The statement asserts itself
"without qualification.")

Too late I discover that fat pockets
show up on fat women whose skin
shrinks as they age
and in no case
has to do with
improper elimination:

Those French masseuses
who pronounce cellulite
a combination of toxic products
in saturated tissues, fat,
and water,
           lie.

Fat is fat is fat.

(Yet the lipectomy expert exhibited pictures
on the t.v. talk show yesterday
of love handles even on starved inmates
of Belsen: heredity, says he. Let me
eliminate it for you . . .

Suddenly, I'm worrying how
references to concentration camps
too often mean, declared a friend, *cheap*
thrills for readers, easy fame
for writers: how Milosz explained
that Polish poets, after the war,
wrote of such things as going to the store.)

The FDA's final remark:
"You can be sure Rubens' nudes
didn't care."

Next day I spend half the morning
in front of the mirror, pinching
and dimpling. Fretting at how ashamed
I am in bathing suits, how if the fat doctors

could see me like this
they'd spot me in a trice
as a victim of vanity
(if not DNA)
and appetite, my guilt
betrayed by habit, attitude and what the FDA calls
"Hard to Budge Pudge," the naked affirmation
of a fate which, had I known
better — on paper, in the restaurant,
at the supermarket — on second thought,
now I'd still dare.

Alice in Gray

Too old for the looking glass,
for the Cheshire games, but still
playing the odds to find
a form for a life:

I'd cant-call this *a mid-life
crisis*, except that exogamous
searching's been my mode since six
(when my favorite book was *Peter Pan*)

or kindergarten — probably the latter:
I remember Mother's stories
(or my own recollections) of how
(at first) I cried and cried, and wanted
only to go home. Then just to go.

So I've gone. And placed my debts
on schools, friends, husbands; Muses —
cities — regions — the prairie,
the desert, the South;

rhyme, even that. Life
for a form, or form
for a Life:

Try me. Try me.
Hands, eyes, ears,
feet, toes. Ligaments.
Corpuscles, brain: open

        Mouth.

◖◗ Coyote, I call you
◖◖◖◖◖◖◖◖◖◖◖◖◖◖◖◖◖◖◖◖

▶▶▶▶▶▶▶▶▶▶▶▶▶▶▶▶▶▶

cure

◖◖◖◖◖◖◖◖◖

Cinquain

◖◗

Someone
Cut the moon in half.
Like a yellow melon
It has scattered golden seed
Everywhere.
　　　　　　　　　—*Clementine Newman*

Delectation

Uncle John
  always
ate his peas
  all

at once (or
whatever; he
never mixed
anything, had
mashed potatoes
first, not with
green beans
and bacon bits

or carrots,
dined on
meat before
bread, or
bread before
meat, whichever

was his order
for the day) —
savored each pea
individually,
with gusto, then
each beet or bean,
each bite of lean
beef or pork
fat, crisped
and crepitant
on top, sweet
and soft
behind —

rebelling against
casseroles,
perhaps,
too many Sunday
socials, pickle juice
sapping fresh
tomatoes, creamed
   corn
   sinking
in the stew —

   or, perhaps,
   asserting
   the simplicity
   of order, clarity,
   material answers
   to single questions
   of arrangement

   — or maybe Uncle John
just liked his peas
the way he liked
his women,

one at a time,
one by one,
rolling round
plump flesh
or wrinkled skin
over his taste buds
slowly, relishing

each fold
and feature,
  bump
or valley,
   turn
and texture,
each part
speaking body
to his tongue,

delighting
in substantial
idiosyncrasy
and loving
every one.

"Anything worth doing is worth doing badly,"

Says the preacher,

such as: 1. praying
        2. cussing
        3. making love.

Child, don't you reckon even Jesus Hisself
had to practice making perfect?
       In Gethsemane
even He must of hollered
"God, You ain't exactly told me
how to do this, how the hell
You expect *me* to save
the whole damn human race?!" —

so when you slip up
and shout AMEN
at the wrong chorus, don't think
you got to ship out; the Devil
ain't picked up nobody yet
that the Lord lifted up
after a fall.

Ugly

"I wouldn't for a minute use language that I think is ugly."
—Diane Wakoski

In Madison, Florida, when you act up
they say you're acting "ugly."

Don't be ugly, Gramma'd say,
be nice. Don't be ugly.

Ugly girls will not do dishes after supper.
Ugly girls will whisper and cut up in church.
Ugly girls go with ugly boys.

And the ugly words were not just words
like "hell." It's not only ugly to pick
your nose, it's ugly to tell somebody
who's doing it "It's ugly to pick
your nose," instead of just

"That's ugly." And it's ugly to tell old Mrs. Parson
in front of the whole Audrey Bevan Circle, loudly,
that her slip is showing. That she's got a run in her hose.

Though slips and runs are ugly.
Though you could say, oh no, I've got
an ugly old run, and excuse yourself.

And you could say things privately
if you said you didn't mean to be ugly.

I don't mean to be ugly, but . . .
that Wilkins boy is purely trash.

If Miss Essie colored her hair
she'd look a whole lot younger.

If that black's natural
so is Mr. Jackson's toupee.

Nice girls had to understand ugly.

So in Madison on Saturday nights
when we were too young to drive cars
we'd just walk together uptown to the show.

It had a front door marked "Us"
and a back door marked "Them."

Now that's what I call ugly.

Table Talk with Spaghetti

for Dottie

George
thinks he's a dog:

only cat I ever knew
who'd escort you out
to the car
and back again,
growl at strangers
and bite, too,
if you didn't watch out:

that cat — a real "attack
cat," not just some slogan
on a doormat — that cat
was *mean.*

So when Alice told me
to look out for George
when I came over that afternoon —
he'd got loose and they hadn't
found him yet — I was ready
for ambush, but never
that big *ker-whap!* of a tail
smashing the elephant ears
by the front door — "Oh, good,"
Alice said, "you found George!
That darned alligator
pulled that chain of his right out
of the ground the other day
when it was too wet to hold it

and he's been hiding ever since.
You know he doesn't have to eat
very often, so he likes to get down
inside the water meter and wait
to scare the meter man" (who'd finally
learned to raise the lid
with a very big stick. This was
in the old days, you understand,
when we had those great big
housings, big enough even for a gator
       like George
to get in, and how was *I* to know
Alice had an alligator and a cat
with the same name? This was Louisiana,
cher, down there

they're everywhere you look.
But he didn't just wander in,
the way they took over the city lake
in Madison five years ago, Alice's
herpetologist son Dave gave them George
once, home for a visit. So they kept him staked
up in the back yard until they finally had to
take him to the zoo — he never hurt anybody
but he just got too big, and it got too
complicated trying to keep him chained
up — trying, once they got him, to keep George
       off of George).

Red Plaid, Black Coffee & a No. 3

Over easy . . . got it. Yeah,
I bet it's gonna be hot again
just like yesterday — say ninety-five
degrees? Well, maybe. And you're looking
for some girl to fan you, but mostly they
just want to fan themselves? Uh-huh.

What, a good day to cool off in a pool? OK,
Darling, look, I'm glad you think I'm hot. But
what *I* got to have is: 1. Myopic. I mean,
a 'lady of a certain age,' it do come in handy
to just say "Hon, this ain't no contact sport,"
or "Great, now take off the glasses." — 2. Knows
how, & likes to laugh at everything. Hey, what's
the point of its all being so serious if you can't
take a poke even at yourself? Is about 75% boy.
Well, OK, 60%. *Maybe.* Feet on the ground
& head in the clouds. & it wouldn't hurt
nothing none if he could sing.

Cure

Lemon juice & honey,
Mother's remedy

for ague, sore throat,
whatever symptoms

wouldn't quite yield
to diagnosis, smooth

devotion I've not made
myself, just think of

sometimes, as if it were
still on my tongue — odd

how that sweet taste
made sharp, tart citrus

made sweet now makes me think
of you — far off

from coming nightfall,
tasteless sorrows

the slate sky rains
past my window (too easy,

too easy, some of them,
to figure). You know how

weeks after the storm
hits, you can still choke up

at the sight of fisted
metal, wind-split foundations

but you don't find 2 words
worth squat to say when someone

introduces you to somebody
who's lost it all & still jokes

like a cavalier about falling
plaster, 50's furniture, an empty house

the family's been lent to live in whose owner
changed nothing, not even the furnace

filter, after the wife died — where's
lemon juice & honey then, literal or

figurative? Tell me if you are
my friend, tell me some other story

I don't already know — say how to make
a red rose grow, tend grief, make it

better, anything, even why I never
should have written you this letter.

"The world is a dangerous neighborhood"
— Dan Rather

So might the inchworm moralize —
unaware of Lebanon —

crooked little body
I picked up on a napkin
mid-progress in my kitchen
across rose petals
spread out to dry. It clung fast

to the flimsy trapeze
when I carried it to the yard
and would not inch off
when I put the napkin on the ground,
unattached end looping back
from the freedom of grass
to the knobbed feel of paper.
I watched its fibrous toehold

a good ten minutes, saw it
marked with a strawberry egg
of excrement no bigger than a pinhole
as red as a rose. Finally
I plucked the worm, gave it
to the beryl-bladed sea.

> (So might I moralize that we too
> inch on the edge, our offal
> however less lovely, our hopes
> on traction but fate determined

by some unobserved
giant, perhaps, who could crush us
at will, would just as soon
mash us as take us
to the garden, might not even
consider remanding our dust
to the rose leaves, though subject
to sudden compunctions — some mistral

      that lifts us
            as easily as grace, as if

we were nothing
at all.)

Nuya Saligugi
(Stone Turtle)

Carved and left by ancient man
in a soapstone quarry near Nottely
River 4 mi. West of Murphy N.C.

If I could know, I do not know

how. Did I come where
I have heard the water sing
of seeding me, strange

voices naming me — something
I must be remembers

deep, earth unfolding. Waking then
to sun. When the cold shadow it was

warmed. You became. Moving
with all I learned to long

for, "flesh"
& "blood," eyes darker

than the darkest leaves
in tree-fall, the black drift

of your hair. They speak
my name now as "stone," a word

I cannot remember. I cannot remember
words from you, only what your edge
kindled into what I never was

nor thought I could be, the likeness
of a creature that lived
& moved as you did, but

differently. But
what I most knew was

your company. And when
you were gone I waited
a long time.

Why do I now hear words
I did not wish to understand,
oh I have forgotten what language it was

you taught me, even the "Cherokee"
name they call me, no, a stranger
tongue. *Coyote*, I call you

though I cannot name you, the words
I do not know burn. Lost
in dry earth, this body

of bone, I am lost
to your laughter, clear
water. I weary

forbearing. & yet it is you
this wind smells of & I
am afraid of, who stole me

to your shaping, I can be
no single thing. Perhaps
I am a jewel

or a rainbow, a blade of grass
or even a woman. Coyote touch me
again & I may become

a cloud

or an egret. Once
more, & I may speak.

night song
◀◀◀◀◀◀◀◀◀◀◀◀◀◀

On the Road
◀▶
The engine's throb
Muffled by the sound of young voices
Singing
Beats out a dim accompaniment
To the melody
Which bears us on golden wings
Over the swift miles.
—*Clementine Newman*

Of Another Stripe

I
(Saturday Night)

We go to a dinner party
   where talk breeds
      skunk tales.

Nora had a squatter
  once, underneath
     her house —

Shirley bunks one still:
they plug the hole, it shoves the bricks,
      pops back in.

De-scent it! Elliott suggests
  (a fulsome, likely pet) —
No sir, cry Shirley, Helen Rose,

pleading the offensive defense.
(Besides, sighs Dick, deodorized, she'd be dead-set
to feed it, nurse it, rescue it from foes.)

II
(Sunday Morning)

In the middle of the night
  I smell skunk.
Go back to sleep, my husband moans,

it's your imagination — so
I do. But when we wake
its wake's so pungent

59

he can't help agree some Mustelid's
        effluvial nocturne's
hazed the atmosphere close by.

Moreover, back from breakfast out,
we find the scent's an inside,
    not an outside, air —

investigate out back, locate
        a gap
in the foundation, left uncovered

by the furnace crew. *Now* what to do?
        — the rapscallion might still be there —
not seal it up inside; not go in after it

to risk malodorous ablutions,
not destroy it . . . what? Left
quizzical for now, we bide

its noisome descant
(or protection), decide
for the moment   not to decide.

Nightrider

Docked in front
of the Krispy Kreme

the squashed chewing gum
wadded to our car's
illuminated hood

opens its eyes
wide, expands into
a tiny frog
trembling
in the neon glare,

aboard, apparently,
since the field-edged shopping-center
parking lot ten miles
and 60 mph down the four-lane
Parkway

if not fallen
from the sky,

holding to
the aqua glaze
as we eat doughnuts
quizzing our odd passenger,
staring past the shocked-pink
message "Hot Doughnuts Now"
through the restaurant looking glass,
asking ourselves
how long

the foreign body
will hang on,

long enough, we hope,
to re-traverse the ten miles
south to grass & water,
dirt & trees

again: strangely oblivious
to alternatives as we leave

the question to our vehicle, bearing
our nervous, greenish
inexplicably attached
tenacious

hitchhiker
from
fluorescent grace

to incandescent speed
traffic of decibels
erratic gusts
and last

a foliated outpost
at the dead-end of a street
backed against a farm tract
bought to be the subdivision's
"future recreation area,"

nudged rump
rappelling
off the hood still
slippery with light

to slip into a field-dark
more comfortable,

object, origin, genus
and species
unknown
to us,

as to the pleasant insects
whose night song
it soon will keep.

Nailed in the Bush

" 'It's just one of those freak things . . .' "

Recuperating in his hospital bed
   from gunshot wounds

     the Senator insists
     he isn't mad

      because
   his friend mistook him
   for a turkey

(out on a Saturday shoot
in the woods outside Jackson
he got dropped
     in the swamp
when his lifetime buddy
spied motion in an oak tree,
misread camouflage suit as feathers) —

though he's lucky he isn't dead.
(He is, however, pocked for good
in several strategic places.
   . . . And can he be sure
said misfiring was altogether a mistake?

Haven't all of us, one time
or another, suddenly found our congress
   less of flock
than alien feather, found ourselves
   secretly praying
for some dead ringer in the brake?)

64

Snake Handlers
for Robert

1

Under the suburban woodpile
that was a favored hackberry
before wind felled it
    you see

a lurking copperhead:
so you take time out
from loading the wood
into your neighbor's truck,

heft the shovel,
strike it dead.

2

You used to hunt snakes for sport
back in the woods of Tennessee.
Especially moccasins: you've told me
how one you shot at but missed
nearly "run right up in the boat,"
how cottonmouths are mean and will attack
without provocation, unlike copperheads

who mate for life, are relatively timid,
nasty if they have to be, but generally
    (like Bartleby)
prefer not to be bothered.

(You didn't miss him on the second shot.)

3

Now her cat Blackie trots in from green space

to Rose's kitchen, dangling a snake he drops
on the tile to play with, which slides away

underneath the dishwasher. Rose calls everyone
she knows, who won't come over to help (except
the elderly landlady, equipped with pliers
and a can of Raid). Barricade it! Jane suggests

by phone. So Rose slams a bookcase board
across the kitchen's opening, feels a little
better, dresses up
for a reception
for two friends just wed.

4

Over their wine Rose tells her troubles
to you, jack-of-all-
rescues, and soon
we're back where that devil Blackie
points his desire. Rose changes
into her "hunting clothes," Blackie
gets put out and you unwind a hanger
to a hook, grapple a tail too slender to pull
without breaking it off, then cast again
successfully, copperhead body now patterning the floor
beside you, coiled around the wire
for dear life

as I slap the sponge-mop down, Rose
follows with the broom, you regain
your feet, then wrap the reptile
in the thickest towel available, refuse
to listen

to my snarled *"Kill it!"* or the other spectators'
tacit agreement, bundle the viper expeditiously
back to the field behind the apartment complex,

trusting you won't get bitten, knowing you're finally
doing a dumb snake a good turn, knowing this
is one copperhead

you won't have to expiate, one innocent
saved from the old black cat's predatory
machinations, one more straggler
returned to the *Feld*, where, you instruct us,

"The little bugger's only trying to make a living,
            just like ever'body else."

Silver Streak

Almost as old
as I am, the Bissell's
sweeper hums up

carpet-fuzz, dirt, grasses, broken
leaves, debris a clumsy, cord-bound
vacuum swallows much less

liltingly. Its murmur
calls up visits
from the Fuller Brush
Man, sample lipsticks
on my 6-year-old
mouth, hand-lotion
pillows & perfume.
I don't remember when

Mother bought the sweeper
from the brush man; it just
was there, making short work
of everyday messes, its name
suggesting the trains we'd take
to Florida, say, New Orleans, a certain
silver sheen on things — surprise

of our last visit home, stationed
in Dad's kitchen closet in spite
of Hoover upright, electric
broom. Now, though old enough
to question lipstick, roles, house

keeping, if trouble, teaching, need or "Love
Makes a Fool of Us All," I still find myself —
despite ' independence,' conveniences
I choose not to give up — singing along

with a good ole country boy's "Nothin' I Can Do
About It Now," the "Ball-Bearing Bisco-
Matic Brush Action" whirring risky
if sweet obbligato.

Rhapsody in Bluegrass
for all the A.S.U. conventioneers

What can you say to the fiddler
whose Sallie Goodin melts

your bones, whose moonstruck tones
and wild-goose rail-slide ride your blood

beyond the farthest maiden's prayer, when Billy
in the low ground harmonizes air to nothing

but the fingers & the fiddle & the bow?

And how say grace to the banjo
whooping the high country of your ear?

To hear is almost to believe
in liberty, to fly away to glory

through the woods with a fox
on the run. Spun up the air

the gray eagle soars

above the rained-
out hay, low

wages, night
shift, sorrow, job

or woman gone. And even Death
wears golden slippers. At this board

lost Indian breaks bread with Old Joe Clark
and in the friended dark the guitar licks

the wolves a howling. Bass & breakdown tune
your neighbor's rhythms to your own, Republican

to Democrat, mechanic to professor, black
to white. By the light of the moon the girls

& boys come out and dance: what to say
to the many who have blessed you

in their wild ecstasy, close
as a mother or a lover to strangers

you will never know? What
to the midnight lunacy that croons:

we will belong to each other still
tomorrow, for here in Sandy Land
we all belong

to the music, every one
of us — but play

it again, Sam, play it again.

◖ ● ◗ *So much of you survives*
◖◖◖◖◖◖◖◖◖◖◖◖◖◖◖◖◖◖◖◖◖◖◖◖◖◖◖◖◖◖

◗◗◗◗◗◗◗◗◗◗◗◗◗◗◗◗◗◗◗◗◗◗◗◗◗◗◗◗◗

We walk entranced within a lane
Of mist that dims our sight;
The veil of fog that holds this spell
Has bound us to the night.

—Clementine Newman
(from "November Enchantment")

a marriage
◀◀◀◀◀◀◀◀◀◀◀◀◀◀◀

Around the Fire

While music blares
Feet are shuffling
Rhythmically.
Raucous voices
Shout harshly
Over bits of cardboard.
In a corner
The fire sings its crackling tune
Unheard
        —Clementine Newman

Poesia

Whatever has brought me to your house again
is something — as in "ear," possibly "smile" —
so basic there's no point in thought, simply
being at the door,

where, like any other settled old friend,
you ask me in for wine and speech

and the impossible breach of days mends
in our talk. I watch you watch the face
that watches you, and will watch
as many times as there are days, and doors,
and ways. Tonight when we walk out
on the porch

there are stars,
the sestina in my blood,
the end-words *blood, steps,*
love, wine, stars, man,

the pulse of steps, the whirr of blood,
the red taste of wine, the smell of love,
white stars cunningly bartered. Ganglion
man. Synapse man.

O love of my eye, humming
    stapes, anatomy.

Sheaves
◐
(A Virginal)

Dry leaves,
it seemed;

the poems for you

circle
coldness, grief, hardship
at closed center. Now, so late

you let me know you want me
in that April way,
as the dogwood wants its blossoms

to open
to the sun,

as the azalea presses unfurled
tongues quivering
to air. Like tongues
of flowers

your words enter
the vessel of my reserve,
coax
the thinned broth
thick again with motes

of longing: uncomb honey
at the opened
center

of this body, whose three buds rise
to you,

to your imagined breath
warming membranous tissue, lips
precipitate on lips

until
not only *body*
but its closed gemmula
soul

open
to your image
as to your body

in a recent dream,
pink bulb of generation
on its root-stem
of desire

ready to flower to rain
or in the nectar of the labyrinth

whose circumference I offer
wholly
to you
in the poem,
as the poem,

as I had given my self,

as I had given myself to you

if
you surmised
Bellerophon

and I
your woman.

Hiatus

Does the sun set the same, the whole world over?
Behind the trees and little houses, tonight,
He flung pennons of blue and faintest pink . . .
        —Clementine Newman ("Query")

Listen:

the dishwasher just stopped.
Birds.   And dogs.

Pink light
haloing a neighbor's tree.

Soon, all the sky I can see will blaze *red*

to silhouette black branches
making way for the stars.

You are somewhere — musing?
Watching trees burn?

These words must serve
as stranger at the grate,

as unquiet knocking in the blue flame
behind your eyes, behind the closed gates
of that garden, your body.

Someone has lost the key
that would unlock my own body's doors
but messages may pass through gates:

Dogwoods, leafed now.
Peonies so heavy

the rain marries them
to the mulched ground.

Iris, bluer than sky,
smelling of humus:

Crickets.   Tree frogs.

The day we met.

Blue jays and scarlet cardinals,

            waiting

(Skeletons; Closets)

... And now your cheekbones mirror mine; they raise
your flesh, form hollows underneath the bone;
the shadow on your cheek, so dark these days
at night, so masculine; the tone —

or lack of tone — of waist, the line
of collarbone through shirt: deep structures, once
inobvious, now pointedly define
my own maison with too much eloquence

(Not *mirror*, figure, simply make me see
myself in you, as I have done always;
pronounce the faithfulness, the perfidy
of time, which furnishes such ateliers):

These motives of our bodies rise above
ours, raze us, mark the tenure of our love.

Traveling (via?) Iceland

Last night it happened again —

you say it: *the second time
in three weeks.* The worst embarrassment
possible for any man. I minimize,

but notice: those wry
muscles at your mouth,
the fear in your eyes.

                     Years ago

at such times

your yokel humor triumphed; tonight, it's
a cold fire burns your eyes . . .

I'd been reading aloud about Iceland.
A dream palace, the man said, *a frozen
wilderland* where the slightest movement
echoes for miles inside its ice-hard
sky-skin. You interrupted his

with your words: "failure" — "old."
    Don't we know more

than your white hair, my sun-
          blotted skin?

You were the one who told Ted — near 90,
circulation the merest thread — he would surely
get better. He did.

For a few years. Whereas I, being as usual
overscrupulous, thought your comfort
a lie, and just smiled. Who's to say

which of us was wrong?

Now, when Dad's sick, I say *Dad,*
you will surely get better. For now,

he has (though we've both seen his foot drag
the garden path,
that once crushed leaves . . .)

Listen: *it will surely get better.* It can happen anytime,
to anyone. For any reason. Never mind.

I still want to go with you
to Australia. Would gladly shuttle up
to Mars, or to the moon.

Go East, go North,

wherever we are is simply on the route.
What has failure to do with landscape?

Eat the map. We'll traverse the snow plain
regardless, in our dreams, in our light hours,

taking whatever skins we've got
to keep off the cold

> *(It is an austere place,* the man said,
> *but beautiful: billions of ice crystals*
> *caught in frozen snow fountains, overflowing)*

Reading, for Distraction

The questions and problems that pushed outward from sonnet endings to lyric closure in general continued to move out toward even broader considerations of closure in all literature, in all art, and finally in all experience. Having bumped into a continent, however, and even having set a flag upon the shore, I realized that I was equipped to explore and chart only a bit of the coastal area. It seemed wise, then, to hold the line at poetic closure.

—Barbara Herrnstein Smith

the critical text: I discover
    how ubiquitous
this problem of "closure"

is: mapping craft,

I'm tangled between the lines
with life; thumbing my intellectual nose
    at grief

I find it hitching the ride.

Or: now that the continent's
bumped me: how to say goodbye
to latitudes and longitudes,
topography of the interior; how end
    investigations
that never — except in the mind — began?

(In other words, forbidden *terra*,
this problem of cartography
is not unique: sorrow, love, desire's
no easier to end or to avoid than dying,
living, any other narration — *Id est*, dark
demesne, if provisioned
    I would still

explore you . . . love-tied as I am,
though, I'll just plant the flag
here: and hope it profits us
to note that, having our own
difficulty closing, we can't help
drawing the line — playing the part
of all literature —

All life?

All art?)

Small Lyric *als Abschied*

Kennst du das Land wo die Citronen blühn,
Im dunkeln Laub die Goldorangen glühn . . .

Do you know Goethe's poem — *kennst du das Land?*
No gold-oranges grow wild in North Alabama country
(though a cherry laurel's rooted in our back yard) —

and certain kinds of lyricism
are ruled outlandish by the quaint recidivism
of our century: but soon it will be Christmas,
in three days you are leaving on a trip
that's supposed to last only a few weeks, yet
you keep repeating "Have a good spring"
as though then you won't be here —

so that there is a place I know of in the mountains
     where, in pines and laurels after frost and snow
     crisp light shines through layers of ice,
     the river crackles in the canyon
     over frozen motes, the lodge-keeper
     sells you firewood if you've paid the rent

where I would take you, *umherschweifenden Freund,*
if only for the day.

After Many Disappointments: Many Deaths

They say you've been depressed for weeks
with "no proximate cause."
But these are just the laws
of grief, I fear; I fear
it's just the pathetic gargoyle opening its jaws
again for one more gulp

never able to digest the mess in one's craw
all at once, and subject to recurrent fits of hunger,
whence it feeds again and yet again,
not in stages so much as phases of satiety
and emptiness, till there's nothing left to gnaw.

(But no. For comfort, what to say?
It's just that such images have helped me, sometimes,
keep the damned thing at bay.)

Rain: Too Much to Say

What I require is
Simplicity: this rain
confuses the streets. It melts
down the windowpanes at your back,

seems to drip through the glass
and adulterate speech: makes
the simple words we say
change character and bleed
against our silkscreened ears
like so much watery ink (We try to speak
plain sentences, but in this moist air
our words run like wash). Don't tell me

you hate wearing glasses
now, hate getting soft
in the knees; I'll stop telling you
I want to move to NC, I want
the body I had at twenty —

What I want is **PRINT**,
bold, black, unmistakable,
Gothic script on an outsized page,

the simple heart,
the simple hand.

The Marriage

1

What has changed? if anything —
since those days when you looked to me
      like nothing so much

as light, when for you to walk into a room
meant only the blind advent of radiant source?

Then I thought (if I thought) of you merely
as enlightened haze, conceived you
only in the mindless blood
that slyly fondles veins or brain.

Is the difference: just the sudden focusing
        of your face

so that one day, climbing your mouth
I traced a small scar?

2

I remember a certain wedding — not
  ours — though our ghosts both
walked the aisles. I remember

thinking "We are too old
for this — bride & groom & we
beyond 'maturity,' prancing
beneath the canopy of dreams
like children" — like the unredeemed
adults who believe the ever after
      we are.

90

Afterward,
we all danced. I notice,
now, such things as
your erratic two-step

your occasional stooped habit
of walking on clear, still days
like an old man in a wind

the way your face has of precipitately shutting
like some caryatid's eyelid. I endure
(complainingly) your constitutional aphasia

regarding the things that matter — seeing them
in your eyes; or, after all these corporeate
years, deeming I'm not without proof
in presumption. *Nuptials,* grandfather
preacher said, *have little to do*

with ceremony: everything with
hierophany: and some priest
or wishman stitched us lives ago
behind our backs, twins knitted heart to head
with celestial (or infernal) thread, moving

in the same internal weather
and capable of breaking necks
        or rubbing noses
with a minor wrench: bound

hand to hand, we stand, blood kin
as if we had slit skin and bled from wrist
    into wrist, breathing in

the dark which is in us, which we are
and now must keep

from our children, light as sunbeams,
transparent as noon, who float
    like moted rays
above the polished floor.

husband death

▶▶▶▶▶▶▶▶▶▶▶

Lights Out

Voices murmur
Drowsily
Tales are told
Of past and future
Wind sighs
Through the tree-tops
Silence
At last.

— *Clementine Newman*

Mutability

Even the starry covenant deceives.
Still, let's be happy to believe
in the figure for a while — there's reprieve.
—Rilke

How to come to terms with the fractal
    force of everything: summoned

by blood and by love,
you leave the blustering prairie
for the ignited South

only to find
no cosmic reprieve

but that in 1964 (and '93)
Sweet Home, Alabama received
18 inches, then a foot of snow,
in 1974 (and '89) a killing
rosary of tornadoes

told on a lesser scale
the years between and since, and today:
 another ice-storm rivaling the one

that left Dad (in Nebraska)
without power for days.

All this . . . *weather,* and psychology too:
not only have physicists found out the apparent
randomness/symmetry (?) of all
of the above,

but each successive grief
(in overcoming, and having overcome which
one is supposed to grow/have grown
    in strength)

hits harder, lasts longer,
recurs to depart
one never knows when or where
or for how long. (The unconscious,
Discover magazine informs us,
is only the beginning. . .)

Not only that:
there seems to be another solar system.

And not only *that* besides: bubbles
    out of the primordial cauldron
    are supposedly still creating universes
strung out like pearls across the sky,
or space, or vastness, whatever nacres

That which apparently is or did come
from what we could call Nothing (since
the basic units of matter, leptons
and quarks, occupy no space),

the invisible grain of sand in the Oyster
        that has flowered anatomically
        and astronomically to become an infinite (?)
        necklace of universes replicating
        according to laws or acausal synchronicities
        as yet beyond our comprehension,

That wears us like ornaments, that ices
birch trees into jewels that fall heavily
and beautifully across roadways,

across telephone wires,
across the robe of frost
burning our red clay lawn.

Afterlife

I have not finished with my dead:
will I never finish

not finished, so long as there are eyes
for photographs, fingers to manipulate
cold jewelry, ears to auricle

underworld echoes. Services of burial
do their job too well: besides
    flowers, I've embedded
coffins: the one I chose, mahogany
lined in blush satin. That haloed
    her moss-rose skin
    will I never forget —

Just look at one
dead face, one
polished lid. The dead
have a way of making

true of you: one moment
you're dreaming *1963*, when you went
with her to the World's Fair in Seattle —
how you read *Hawaii* in every available
line, refusing absolutely to speak.
The next it's the moment she last spoke to you, coming
conscious two minutes long enough. *(Oh)*
    They possess many such

coffins, these precocious "deceased":
getting ahead of themselves even in
premature reincarnations, fleshed
    out before their time — stepping

backward through the doors of high schools, sporting
crinolines under formals in ballrooms, and when one
who is still alive wonders 'if they do that jitterbug thing
at Cornell now' — a place you never saw him — he materializes
in the ghost dance behind his left shoulder
as a young man, handing down the dance-step in all
            their macaronic ways. Some,
like him, you have appropriated or made
out of someone else's memories, created doubles
of — say — old friends of your husband's
you never met, propagating images that multiply
like homunculi, famished
to consume your world.

Some inform you loquaciously
of every trip they ever made,
itemizing salient points West.

Others stand silent, biding their time.

A few live only in the irises
that ironicize you out of the mirror,
in the lines that show, nose to chin, the exact
passage of your smile, that disappearing Houdini

which soon enough will take up residence
in some new tomb.

Suicides

— numbering them again:

Sylvia Plath, Anne Sexton. Susie's father
unexpectedly, when we were 13. Cilla.
Judy's Joe, the night he got maudlin drunk
and rebellious, decided to slice his wrists
just to see what she would do. Then he got scared.
    Also, Marilyn
    Monroe, and Sonny:
who sold cars: and Fletcher, political success
story (local; inner city track). Obviously not merely
Hollywood, not typically female: have you looked,
really looked at those two eyes that stare at you
over toothpaste every morning — how do you know
you might not suddenly remember where you hid the gun?

Crash out your poor brains, numb anyway
at 6 AM, and let them drool all over
the bathroom tile, fizzing and dribbling
for your wife to find when she calls you
to breakfast — then sees you carried out on a stretcher?
Hear ye, hear ye, borderline people: Count the manifest ways:
pills, jumping out of airplanes, flying off bridges, making fire
with knives, running under trains: *oh blessed marble,*
smooth foxy silencer of the silent night . . . and our

Joe too. Good old Joe, lived out a car wreck
that rebuilt his face, survived divorce, licked
alcohol, then came home to find his second wife
stiffening slowly, garishly, from somebody
else's (?) mayhem . . . Sordid, yes —

but true. People in Boston, Bishop and Valdosta: all
true. True in spite of children or jobs. Even love.

    Deus. Dei. Domine.

Show us some better way out.

Beethoven and the Man at the Omaha Train

> ... his figure towers like a colossus astride the two centuries.
> —Donald Jay Grout *(A History of Western Music)*

My ears have been stopped for four weeks.
It's the clinic for you, says the doctor.
Surgery, too, if you're not to be deaf.

i

The boy rode the coach at twenty-one
From Bonn, a journey of five hundred miles
Or so, to Wien — Vienna — then a run
Of a week by stage. He learned the styles

Of Haydn, Mozart, wrote nine symphonies
to Haydn's hundred, Mozart's fifty, yet (no doubt)
"A colossus," "looms across two centuries" —
One agrees with Donald Grout.

The man's deafness began in '98,
Just some six years beyond the ride from Bonn.
He wrote off the "hot terror" of his fate
Until '27: then (not 60) he was gone.

Not Classic nor Romantic, Grout explains:
"He is Beethoven." What was, remains.

ii

I can't hear my watch tick in my right ear.

The Shea Clinic's waiting room is full: "Plan to spend the whole day
waiting," advised a friend whose child's eardrums they'd replaced.
(The same day, a neighbor who has been here — unsuccessfully —
confided she's had no hearing in her left ear since childhood mumps.
She assured me — truly, I wouldn't have known it — she does *well enough*.)

100

Strangely quiet, children mumble to each other against one wall.
A row or two ahead, a stylish matron laments the uncertain balance
that has plagued her for years. "She says she's planned suicide
more than once," confides the airline stewardess whose job depends
on the ear that — after "simple" dental surgery — went
tinny, then dead. *"Only my art"* (declared Beethoven) *"held me back."*

iii

Nothing held back the man who once wished to go
With me to Kansas, who saw me waiting for the train.
Not my diamond, face up where it would show
On my left hand; my sketchbook; not the pains

I took to remain an hour in the station's restroom —
There he sat. Tired, taught "kindness," I let him buy
Me coffee, proclaim again how we could zoom
To Kansas City in his pickup, fly

Low enough to make the all aboard
On the Southern Express bound for my fiancé.
He did escort me to my coach, without a word,
Kissed me suddenly before it pulled away . . .

Had he found in fantasy a way to live
Less lonely, imagining a love no one could give —

iv

Or was he — no "colossus," but big, a beefy man hard
not to notice — no romantic, just some farmer out looking
in the best place and way he knew of to catch a pretty girl,
an ordinary man, no Son of Sam, no classic circumstantial wreck,
not trapped on Nebraska dirt generous enough to fodder a six-foot
belly, but not a soul: — just someone unknown, whose unmitigated

persistence oddly reassures me now, waiting
for my turn on the machine that reads how much
loss, how much longer . . . whose minuet of faith

you, too, might appreciate, "great Mogul," melancholic
ironist whose *Eroica* I can hear even now, will hear
even *if*, even *then* — you, Beethoven, "one of the great
disruptive forces in the history of music," whose control,

like his perhaps, depended on no patron and no public,
who wooed the ideal audience and so wrote, finally,
to save us: in the shape of himself.

Intimacy

to the memory of Virginia R. Murray

Like the poems that inspired us, we were
occasional friends — meeting at workshops,
at the Christmas or winter readings; at the banquet, authors'
luncheon, or the lecture; at the Southern conference.

Once, when you needed a ride and I couldn't leave town
till afternoon, you beguiled a hundred miles of morning
with my enchanted husband; another time, you and I made
a giddy triolet with my neighbor six streets over, your best friend.

We never had picnics on the mountain, didn't talk much
on the phone, didn't meet for lunch, never went wildflowering
or walking, didn't go to school together, didn't have children
who went to school together, did almost nothing together
except most of everything concerning poetry. Yet to us,
                    poetry was everything.

When I heard you'd left, ill, for your daughter's
in Birmingham, I'd kept those cards and letters
flying South, as you had always sped them, by
local post, to me *(what a treat it was to be with you . . . ignoring
of my mortality . . . I wish I had the words . . . blessed . . .*) Heart-sick

how long? a decade? you'd laughed at bones' frailty as at the shingles
that had given you a silver wig, or at my slender jokes, giggling —
a head shorter in silks and cameos — like a champagne flute
struck to liquid gold. I never heard you utter
one harsh line, or word to anyone.

When I got home from Carolina that June weekend
to find via answering machine that you had died,
and couldn't leave our guest, Mom, Alzheimer's restless, alone
the next day to go to your funeral —

I knew you'd understand: but I felt — mortified, lost
without formal closure. Longing for it and for you,

Estate Sale Day I sought comfort in the house
I'd been to those few times, then got only so far as
the crowded kitchen where your jewelry was laid
before my own heart (or will) gave out. And now, invited
back by my neighbor, your in-law, our friend, to choose books
from books left from the aftersale, I buzz like some *paparazza*

through your rooms: the kitchen where, furious
at your anonymity, I'd reproved the clutch of women
appraising your costumery (*"nothing good left"*— *I saw her
wearing that);* the dining space where poets laureate
savored canapés and coffee; the carport where I nearly
snatched one of your signed chapbooks out of the thieving hands
of a book-dealer — the empty living room; hall, bedrooms,

unsuspected den. Amid its remaindered confusion I scour
floor-stacks, cartons, half-winnowed built-ins for your name,
the names, the words of friends: *for Virginia, old correspondent
in the Poe world; to Virginia ("I cannot sleep —")* claiming enough volumes
to bring my hall-shelf's 'special collection' of your books — bookplated,
annotated, stuffed with dated clippings — to eighteen. *Anthology
& Yearbook of Magazine Verse & American Poetry, American Poetry
Anthology, Negative Capability, Designed for Reading, The World Treasury
of Modern Religious Thought* . . . translated by death

to artyfacts (you'd laugh at that) — like the ebony-handled
coffee urn on a console I'd forgotten, or never seen, keys
on keys, the prosperity pin-with-legend of yours I bought,
then gave away, the flowered mug of yours I bought,
then gave away, those eighteen books of yours less one

I gave away, green glass (?) ring in foam block and marbled paper
I bought, can't wear, and will not give away, faux pearls that may
or may not arrive with me at the symphony — high-heeled
shoes on the dinette in near-new boxes, an astonishing 7 ½
royal blue, fire engine red.

What's more, from some drawer where you'd put them aside,
our friend confides to my booksatchel with your books
ziploc after amazing ziploc of "Fifth Prize Publicity Sweepstakes"
presentation stones, accrued like polished verses: *Tamiz emeralds,*
Guaranteed genuine as per accompanying Certificate
      of Authenticity; Black Stars of India —

Oh Virginia . . . if the walls could talk.

After Sylvia

When they come to pick my remains —
Noh-masks pious in *aprés*-author ritual

I will not be there — will have vanished
with the fat complacence of that famous
Cheshire Cat — or say, for science, I've
had myself cremated — translated

right out of Auschwitz in a puff of purple smoke.
No journals. There will be no letters from Sivvie
to Mama, no agonies sizzling over
telephone wires or on tapes that,
too few, too soon stop. No diaries,
no *billets-doux,* no body

by the gas jet — no blood congealing
like consommé in cleanly slashed veins
(*pace, Nosferatu,* I shall be quite dead).

Someone may discover
grocery lists — "bacon" or "mayonnaise"
crossed off neatly — beneath a Kleenex
at the bottom of a cast-off purse. Worn-out shoes, records
of entertainments, keys to unknown but somewhere
existent locks. There will be calendars, perhaps
scribbled notes — also postcards — revealing my whereabouts
on various given dates. There will be — and I expect thanks
for this — mss. of all descriptions, neatly labeled folders,
rough drafts liberally revised — and (but only sometimes)
dated (*bitte sehr, Genosse*) — as for

the rest, I've buried my more tumid secrets
in the sky, sent them — ember-crisps of
amateur pyrotechnics — wisping off into the robin's-egg air:

Let them make a life of that.

Let them, Xacto knives in hand,
have at the corpus with abandon —
let them lay the fibers bare: or,

with the élan of any garden rainbow,
let them scan the seven pairs of eyes
that presided, all unknowing, over my
peripatetic destiny —

the seven lashed seas, the seven
ecstatic hills, the seven orbits
of a cerulean, carnally avid, manifestly
dark and jealous God.

Engagement

Goodbye, goodbye!
There was so much to love, I could not love it all;
I could not love it enough . . .

"It looks like Venus," said the friend I first
showed Grandma's imperfect diamond

to . . . "or the moon, between
two stars." The 'stars'

were brother Walden's gift
to the brave sister he loved

best, to consecrate an uncommon
twelvemonth of her life, daring higher

education amid red clay & Spanish moss.
But when Audrey Ellie Bevan came home

from that first year of college to the sand
of Madison, Florida and saw

John Jordan Newman, come
from Georgia

to live & work with his relations at
Smith's Hardware on Main Street,

she stayed home.
A woman of her time

and in love, just 2 months
& 2 weeks shy of 18

she married her dark
and handsome man.

Who could have told her
but chance & grief

she'd lose him
and Walden too,

Jay first to t. b., then
Walden two years later

in the influenza epidemic of 1918?
But before she'd had to have

John Jordan Newman
chiseled on the stone

beside her stone beside her mother's stone
in the first row

of the Newman lot in Oak Ridge
fronting her two daughters

and my father,
facing the back row

where her ward, Joe, & Auntie Wilson
preside,

Jay had built her
one of the finest houses in Madison

where she then let rooms.
On that & the rent

from 3 other houses he'd had sense & money
to buy & the income from her Daddy's farm,

with her widowed mother's help,
with "help" from the other side

of town,
she did

what she had to do
& raised two girls

who proved her love of learning
in their Masters' degrees

and lives and in my mother's children.
No Miss Havisham, on that October day

Jay Newman died, my Grandma burned
her white dress as a sacrifice,

then had his diamond set
with Uncle Walden's

in the ring she never took off
and went on with her passionate

life through two World Wars, Korea,
Vietnam, Depression, astonishing t. v. views

of the first humans landing on the moon.
2 years after that "giant step," she lost

her younger daughter to Madame
Cancer, & knew again the folly

of betting on the odds of 'normal'
expectation; the pall

of being, spiritually, dispossessed: although until the last
my uncle's honored guest, of the house — Jay's house —

she'd given, against their and all considered
advice, to that daughter and her husband

when her career girl married, finally,
at 50. Both these Audreys I have to thank

for my middle name and taking lessons
of stubborn if not always wise independence

110

and fear, fear of the one thing Grandma feared most
that I feared most long before she taught me:

Nothing else matters so long as you have your mind.
At last, hers went wayward, hying back

to Little Audrey, back to Mama, back
to Jay. True to the end, though, she defied

& denied the nursing home by dying
while Dad was driving me

from the Omaha airport to the house she'd been
my mother's patient in for six months, leaving

unbroken
my last image of her: the American

Beauty she wore on her long black gown
and its sweep on the mansion stair

in Madison, soaring toward
a local wedding, herself a bride

in ebony, a midnight rose.

A woman like my Grandma knows
what she wants. *I never loved another man,*

was all she said. She waited
nearly sixty years for her J. J. Newman,

and on that August day when at last
she saw him again, I inherited

her ring. Husband Death:
I'm thinking of having the stones

reset. One life's forfeiture
is enough. I know we are

only, blissfully
human,

and I would not, nor would I have anyone
I love be, so alone. And yet

I do sing Ave every day of my life
for you, oh blessed and last teacher

among men: your necessary offices of
burying, the heart's strange

resurrections. Who's to say
there is no joy in solitaire?

I know,

by sorrow & by charity
I am beginning to know

in all the ways that count

she may not have been alone
at all. Hallelujah! Here's

to freedom! And faith, and
chance: uncertainty; giving up

the ghost, the need to finish
or rewrite the story.

Two Views of Howard's Chapel

a memorial to Sallie Howard
constructed by Col. Milford W. Howard
at the North entrance of De Soto State Park, Ft. Payne, 1930's

i

There is this huge
knuckle of God — at least
somebody thought so — em-
braced by a chapel. Somebody

built the building right around
one of the biggest rocks you've ever seen.
It's huge: way higher than a woman's
head: and outside, the cross-topped jagged block looks
like some — I don't know what — some stone-
skinned hybrid out of "Star Trek" — devouring
civilization like a cinema sarsen.

Really, who'd conceive a ridiculous thing like that?
At least it attracts the tourists —
and campers, I suppose,
on Sunday morning, all sweaty
from hiking the river path
to get there, in muddy jogging shoes
and dusty jeans. Their jaws must drop wide

open when they see the whole back wall and altar's
        the behind of Old Granddaddy Rock
(They must think: "It takes an Alabama redneck!") —

There's some verse or other on it
out of the Bible, or something. Seriously,

you ought to see it — we'll run up
next time you visit —

those little yellow flowers by the doorstep — I've never
been sure of their name — ought to be out
about April. And the churchyard — it's so quiet there —
blooms halfway to heaven, this time of year.

ii

IMMORTALITY

God Has All Ways Been As Good To Me As I Would Let Him Be

When the rough pines burr
their wind songs
God's just clearing His throat

& if His funnel bell should sweep
the mountains clean
eventually   He will make them new

new trees, new mountains   All things
the Lord hath made
& unmade He shall remake

Take me into your heart oh God
the stony fist
schist chrysalis

and cupped hand budding
to silk-brush   & a burst
of seed   Lord

conceive me   bear me
as the child
who would be found

Lord, I pray make me happy.
But God don't let me forget how I cried

Requiem (Remembering Vardamon)

i

The funeral director demurred.
The relatives looked askance.

But Mother wouldn't have the ministrations
of the cosmeticians: no
        stitching dead flesh
           to shape as if it breathed,
no wax museum hairdo, no drained veins,
no Sunday spectators paying
their Last Respects: she'd had enough of that —

ii

seen enough dead faces, red, rouged, painted —

closed enough dead eyes
smiled enough at wives
           and the husbands the children the cousins
           the sisters the brothers the neighbors
who came, went, filled the guest book, exclaimed
how amazing, how *Just Like She Was.*

iii

As a child she had seen them

in a live-oak county town
where weddings, funerals, *affaires*
were served up with the fish

on the silvered buffet of a most
proper hostess, in most proper
mansions. Corpse or fish —

115

was it all the same?
They gossiped all the same.

iv

It was not the same
when she'd married away

to a literary whirl
where intellect was "Free,"
where at her bridge table

one discussed Proust, not Peter
next door. Though the mansions grew
smaller, the air

waxed larger, filled with the aroma of Bach, profundities,
fish basted with a sauce from Paris.

It was not the same?

v

They died all the same.

So we sit in a funeral parlor
in the county town,

my father, a closed casket, my brother
            and me

where the wives the husbands the children
the cousins the sisters the brothers —

the undertakers —
are puzzled. *Not even
a look?*

They don't see.

vi

My mother is a fish.

*My mother is a fish swimming
and swimming*

in a dark, secret sea.

vii

In the next room lies a corpse.

Its cheeks and lips pinked; its hair
stiffed *just so.* On the air,
        a faint whisper

of *My Sin.* Mourners close
in to see the revamped body:

It looks lifelike.

Es lächelt.

(It smiles.)

Vista

*I will wait for you, I will come to lead you across
the bridge of night into the meadows . . .*
—Jean Humphrey Chaillie

Raised on Nebraska prairie, now claimed by red clay,
I think of death as a place, a prospect inhabited

by many friends: among them Grandpa Theodore, Grandma
Newman; Grandmother Militzer, who died before I was born,
my mother's father, who died of t. b. in 1916; Jane, Ed, Cilla,
Jeffrey, my three students killed in a car, my mother, my father,
Uncle Mal, aunts, my husband's grandparents, who would have
welcomed me if they had known me, his father, Ted, Wendy,
Eldrice, Virginia, three Joes, Greg Andrews, who called me *Ave,*
        my biggest crush in junior high:

Somehow they all got through the door, have gone before me
as I will go before you, the not yet born:

thinking of them, of you — of friends in verse
like brooding William Cowper, whose words
        (But what is commentator's happiest praise?
        That he has furnish'd lights for other eyes,
        Which they who need them use, and then despise)
have soothed the viewless evenings — or reading the landscape
of Cowper's Yardley Oak, *A shatter'd veteran, hollow-trunk'd*
perhaps, like the grandfather hackberry, near-bereft
of leaves, we will soon have to cut down —
        and trying to imagine Paradise

I can't: except as *valley, mountain, river, river of stars*
if not "meadows," not "Heaven" *(A huge throat*
                calling to the clouds for drink) —

perhaps death will reveal nothing,
or nothing we can dream of, just
— a difference, life still, if not a life

we can know: perhaps worms will feed
where someone has laid my hardwood coffin,
perhaps someone, you, will remember me.

Perhaps not —

does it matter: if 'there are no more minutes
in all of eternity than there are in say, one minute'?

Yes or no, it is my brief that friends are out there
making the territory habitable, offering us light
and water and shade, that, however it happens,
whenever, in joy, indifference, utter despair, we will
come to them

and so may think of night, of ending, not as *enemy*
or *friend* but both, and neither, not as disconnection
but continuity, the logical outcome; so that

if the night seems long and dark, then
let us do what we can to keep it in its place
and yet not fear the night: I will be there,
oh beloved;
                    we all will.

Epilogue: After Her Father's Death

I once gave you a book
'for the sake of happy memories.'

It was not the gift I'd've given,
had I known better how to give you
what was most in my heart
to give: so much undone

in love and exasperation,
reverence and anger,
I want the centripetal . . . so much
held back, so much unsaid . . . Now,

daily, I see your likeness
through the study door

in little-girl pictures of myself
    which,
with the rest of family,
I have framed and put on the wall:
mourn it in grandchildren not to be born,
children you will not see, now —

Regardless, so much of you survives
in the woman I have become
that wherever you are, or I am
    or will be

will not be sufficient distance,
I both fear and hope,
to efface the transfer

(And now I give myself words
    to live by, hoping
eventually some centering
will hold. But for you,

gone soul so far away — and maybe
     mum to me forevermore,
I'd have struck a better offering
than that chary book I gave you
then, some embrace, some ritual,
some ceremony that would show you to yourself
     irrevocably dear, crossed
though we always were, and for all that

written into my bones, the stony platen
I would not now polish smooth if I could,

     and I cannot).

Notes

"Revocation," page 9: "*Their music . . .*" : quoted from Ernst Curtius, *European Literature and the Latin Middle Ages* (trans. Willard R. Trask).

"Dowry," page 25: "Dowry" was inspired by a family story told to me by Christina de la Torre. Though it is fictional in nearly all respects, some details were suggested by the narratives of Trumbull White, *United States in War with Spain and the History of Cuba* (Chicago and Philadelphia: International Publishing Co., 1898), and Eliza Moore Chin McHatton Ripley, *From Flag to Flag: A Woman's Adventures and Experiences in the South During the War, in Mexico, and in Cuba* (New York: D. Appleton and Co., 1889). "The burning // lava / of a song" comes from Elizabeth Barrett Browning's *Aurora Leigh*, V. 213-14 ("But still, unscrupulously epic, catch / Upon the burning lava of a song"). The war referred to in the last lines is The Ten Years' War, ended in 1878 by the Pact of Zanjón.

"Rhapsody in Bluegrass," page 70: On the first weekend of October, Athens State University (Athens, AL) hosts the Tennessee Valley Oldtime Fiddlers' Convention, which draws enthusiasts from across the U.S.A. and includes contests in numerous traditional categories, from buckdancing or oldtime band and bluegrass banjo down. Fourteen traditional tunes often heard there are named (or, in one case, alluded to) within the poem.

"Hiatus," page 80: "Stranger at the grate": "In all parts of the kingdom these films [leaves of ash trapped against the hearthgrate] are called *strangers* and supposed to portend the arrival of some absent friend." —Samuel Taylor Coleridge, note to "Frost at Midnight."

"Small Lyric *als Abschied,*" page 87: *Umherschweifenden Freund* may be translated as 'my rambling friend.' *Als Abschied:* 'as farewell.' *Kennst du das Land . . . :*
> Knowst thou the land of flowering lemon trees?
> In leafage dark the golden orange glows . . .
> ("Mignon," trans. Christopher Middleton)

"The Marriage," page 90: "corporeate": corporeal; corporate.

"Engagement," page 108: "*Goodbye, goodbye . . .*":
   Some things I overlooked, and some I could not find.
   Let the crystal clasp them
   When you drink your wine, in autumn.
      —Louise Bogan, "After the Persian" (v)

"Two Views of Howard's Chapel," page 113: "some verse or other": "words from Sallie's last letter . . . printed upon a huge beam above." The chapel is a reproduction of the "Wee Kirk 'O the Heather" in Forrest Lawn Cemetery, Glendale, California (where Sallie Howard is buried), itself a copy of the Annie Laurie Church in Scotland. (Dekalb Baptist Association brochure)

"Mutability," page 95: The epigraph translates lines from Rilke's *Sonnets to Orpheus*, 11:   *Auch die sternische Verbindung trügt.*
            Doch uns freue eine Weile nun,
            der Figur zu glauben. Das genügt.

"Vista," page 118: William Cowper (1731-1800) is quoted from a copy of *The Poetical Works: Complete Edition* (London and New York: Frederick Warne, n.d.), awarded to Fred Moss, "for attendance and good conduct," by Christadelphian Sunday School Heanor, Christmas, 1900. 'No more minutes': a "mathematician" quoted by Kathleen Norris in *Dakota: A Spiritual Geography*.